Abe

RAMON BENNETT

SHEKINAH

JERUSALEM

ISBN 978-1-943423-20-0

Published in the United States by Shekinah Books LLC

Distributed in Israel by: Ramon Bennett,
P. O. Box 37111, Jerusalem 91370.
eMail: armofsalvation@mac.com.

Shekinah Books LLC
A division of *Arm of Salvation Ministries,* Jerusalem.

This paperback is subject to discounts for orders of 10 or more
copies when purchased through Shekinah Books LLC. *Abe*
is also available as a Kindle e-Book or in PDF form. Further
information can be obtained, and purchases of multiple hard
copies or single PDF purchases may be made, by logging onto:
http://www.shekinahbooks.com. All listed titles in this book are
available for purchase on *Amazon.com*

*And the Scripture was fulfilled which says, "**Abraham believed God, and it** was accounted to him for righteousness." And **he was called the friend of God*** (James 2:23).

CONTENTS

The Lord Jesus Christ is the most important figure ever to appear in all of human history, and he is the most mentioned person in the Bible. The life, death, and resurrection of Jesus from the grave, changed everything man ever knew, or thought he knew, about God, salvation, and life after death.

KING DAVID

KING David is the next person to be so frequently mentioned in the Bible, and God Almighty said of David, *I have found David the son of Jesse, **a man after My own heart**, who will do all My will* (Acts 13:22). David brought Israel to its pinnacle of historical greatness and his name is mentioned in twenty-eight out of the sixty-six books of the Bible. King David is remembered for his cleaving to God, his military prowess and, unfortunately, his failings in fidelity to his wife and failure with the raising of his family.

David committed adultery with Bathsheba (2Samuel 11:4), and when Bathsheba found herself to be pregnant with David's child, David attempted to cover his sin by having her husband Uriah murdered

(2Samuel 11:14–15). Amnon, one of David's sons, raped his virgin half-sister (2Samuel 13:11–14), and when David heard about the vile deed he did nothing, he was merely *"angry"* (2Samuel 13:21). David's son Absalom declared himself king in opposition to his father, gathered half of Israel's huge fighting force together in an attempt to kill David and overthrow him, his kingdom, and his mighty men. David was forced to flee for his life from Jerusalem, and ran like a rabbit. And when David's mighty men defeated Absalom's troops and killed Absalom—against David's explicit command—David covered his face and cried out with a loud voice, *"O my son Absalom—my son, my son Absalom—if only I had died in your place! O Absalom my son, my son!"* (2Samuel 18:33).

When David grew old and was confined to bed, another of his sons, Adonijah, proclaimed himself king and David never so much as *rebuked him at any time by saying, "Why have you done this?"* (1Kings 1:6).

David had a heart for God and was a hero on the battlefield, but a moral failure in the home. He died in the arms of a stranger, a beautiful virgin girl named Abishag (1Kings

1:1–4)—David was only seventy years old when he died. (2Samuel 5:4).

Israel's great military king, his life, battles, exploits, deeds and moral failures, are spread over fifty-eight chapters of the Old Testament. And *David, after he had served the purpose of God **in his own generation**, fell asleep and was laid with his fathers* (Acts 13:36).

ABRAHAM

ABRAHAM is the third most oft-mentioned person in the Bible and he is the only person whom God Almighty deemed to call his *friend*. Not once, but three times!—(2Chronicles 20:7; Isaiah 41:8; James 2:23). Abraham was God Almighty's *friend*, and God was so impressed with Abraham that not only does he call him his *friend*, but used men, inspired by the Holy Spirit, to connect Abraham with faith and righteousness more than three hundred times throughout twenty-eight books of the Bible, but these twenty-eight books are a twenty-eight different books from those that mention King David.

In contrast to David, Abraham's entire life is chronicled in just fourteen chapters, from the time he is begotten by his father Terah

(Genesis 11:26) until his death at **one hundred and seventy-five years of age** (Genesis 25:7), **an old man, full of years and satisfied with life** (Genesis 25:8). Abraham is always referenced together with faith and belief, and if Abraham's life had been spread over fifty-eight chapters like King David's, references to Abraham would likely have matched the number for those of Jesus. David served *the purpose of God in his own generation*, but Abraham has served the purpose of God Almighty in every generation. He is considered the Father of Faith and for more than two thousand years Abraham has, like Jesus, been held up as an example for Christians to emulate. And also like Jesus, Abraham walked before God and mirrored the faith of God.

Why would God Almighty move to bring Abraham's name to our attention so many times, especially in the gospels and other New Testament writings, if he were not trying to get **_our_** attention, trying to tell us something? Abraham's faith was built on confidence in his God; it was the response of his soul to the revealed character of his God. Faith is more than mental acceptance. It is the mother of hope.

IN this short book we shall look at the life of Abraham, look at his character and see why Abraham was the only person whom God chose to call his friend, and the only person to have physically walked and talked with God Almighty.

BIBLE CHARACTERS HAD MANY OF OUR OWN TRAITS

THE first point I would like to make is that we all need to identify with Bible characters. We are all too often so quick to judge the characters that God saw fit to lay open to scrutiny. I am firmly convinced that in every Christian brother there is a little of Samson and a little of David, and in every Christian sister a little of Jezebel and a little of Bathsheba. I am also convinced that in every brother there is some of Moses, some of Elijah, and some of Boaz. And in every sister there is some of Ruth, some of Deborah, and some of Mary, the mother of Jesus.

GOD'S REVELATION TO US IS DETERMINED BY OUR CHARACTER

THE second point I want to make is that God Almighty is not partial to people.

Deuteronomy 10:17 tells us that the Lord our God is *God of gods and Lord of lords, the great God, mighty and awesome,* **who shows no partiality** *nor takes a bribe.* There is nothing we can offer to God, apart from our entire self, that would induce him to show favor to us. Favor by way of blessing, not by way of favoritism. In Acts 10:34–35, we read of Peter being in the house of Cornelius, and declaring: *"I perceive that* **God shows no partiality.** *But in every nation* **whoever fears him and works righteousness is accepted by him."** No doubt there will be a number of nations represented by my readers, and everyone who fears God Almighty and does what is right is sure of a warm and wonderful welcome from God.

God does not prefer one son or one daughter above another son or daughter. There are no favorites in God's household and Ephesians 2:19 tells us that we are *members of the household of God.* Some people find God in a way that others do not. God Almighty is not partial and he shows no favoritism, therefore the difference lays not with God, but with us. I have said elsewhere that our God is quite beyond comprehension—he is not restricted by boundaries, he is here, there, and everywhere—there is no place and can be no place where God is not. It is the way that we live and act and speak that causes a person to say that God is "far away," or for God to say, *"My friend."* God's revelation to me is determined by my character, not God's.

No One is Perfect Except God
HIMSELF

THE third point that I want to establish is that we do not have to be perfect to win the friendship of God. Too many people feel that God Almighty will not use them or that they will never find favor with him because they are too imperfect. I said earlier that we need to identify with Bible characters. We would be hard pressed to find more than a handful of Bible characters that is not recorded as doing some dumb thing somewhere along the way. They were human just like we are human, but the good news is that God *is mindful that we are but dust* (Psalms 103:14)

Abraham should be a great encouragement to us all, he is called *the friend of God,* but at times he acted as if God never existed. Abraham was not perfect by any means. He made one of the most far-reaching mistakes of all of mankind in that he "helped God out" by having a child by Hagar, his wife's Egyptian maid. Thousands of years later Abraham's work of the flesh continues to war against the work of the Holy Spirit. The wild and lawless character of Ishmael's descendants have provoked endless conflicts with Abraham's progeny of promise, and the conflicts continue until today. No work of the flesh is recognized by God and Ishmael was not recognized by God Almighty as Abraham's heir. Works of the flesh are a pain in God's heart and a pain in mankind's neck. When there is a far-reaching work of the flesh, God Almighty—seemingly as a matter of policy—always raises up a monument to it, placing it before the world to be remembered for posterity.

Abraham got Hagar when he went down to Egypt. There was a severe famine in the land of Canaan, which God Almighty had just covenanted to give to Abraham and his descendants. Abraham believed the Lord for the land, but did not believe him to provide sustenance in the famine, thus he went down into Egypt to forage. How many of us believe God for the extraordinary, but think we need to use common sense for everything else?

Abraham convinced his wife Sarai—before God changed her name to Sarah—to say that she was only his sister. It was a half-truth, because she was in fact his half sister. But a half-truth is also half a lie and lies are sin, and sin always brings trouble to the person who sins and very often to the completely innocent—*and be sure your sin will find you out* (Numbers 32:23). Abraham brought trouble upon Pharaoh by God's hand and got himself and all those with him deported.

Abraham did not learn from that experience in Egypt, he repeated the same deception with Abimelech, king of Gerar. Abraham again said of Sarah his wife, *"She is my sister."* And Abimelech, king of Gerar, was very much taken with Sarah's beauty, *he sent and took Sarah* (Genesis 20:2) and would have slept with her had God not intervened and said to Abimelech, *"Indeed you are a dead man because of the woman whom you have taken, for **she is a man's wife**"* (Genesis 20:3). Needless to say, Abimelech was far from amused at Abraham's deception and said, *"What have you done to us? How have I offended you, that **you have brought on me and on my kingdom a great sin?** You have* *done deeds to me that ought not to be done"* (Genesis 20:9). Even though Abraham was one hundred percent in the wrong, because of God's intervention he came out of the altercation with Abimelech smelling like roses.

Abimelech restored *Sarai* aka *Sarah* to Abraham and also gave him *sheep, oxen, and male and female servants* (Genesis 20:14), and said to Sarah, *"I have given your brother **a thousand pieces of silver;** indeed **this vindicates you** before all who are with you and before everybody." Thus she was rebuked* (Genesis 20:16). Sarah was rebuked because she went along with Abraham's deceit in saying he was her brother. It cost Abimelech *a thousand pieces of silver* to show everyone that he had not defiled Abraham's wife.

Obviously, both Abraham and Sarai had a problem with telling the truth, stretching it instead of relying on God Almighty to protect them. Apparently, this ability to tell half-truths when convenient was in Abraham's DNA, because his son Isaac and his wife Rebekah did the exact same thing to Abimelech (Genesis 26:6–10) and with the same results and the same rebukes.

I can almost guarantee that you and I have, at some time or other, said (at least to ourselves), "Oh boy, I did the same dumb thing again." Like Abraham, we have a tendency to help God out when he seems to be slow in doing what we want done in the amount of time we have allotted for him to do it. It is utter impertinence and reeks of faithlessness, yet we sometimes repeat the same thing a time or two before we learn to move on in our walk with God.

Like Abraham and Sarah, and Isaac and Rebekah, we are not perfect, but we do learn after a while and we do progress. Abraham progressed to be called *the friend of God* and we will take a look at his positive behavior than won him than friendship.

DO NOT BE AFRAID TO LEAVE THE FAMILIAR BEHIND

IN Genesis 12:1 God Almighty tells Abraham (while he was still called Abram) to leave Ur of the Chaldeans and go to a land that he would show him. God also says to Abraham at that time that he will give that land—the land of Canaan—to Abraham's descendants forever. It is interesting to note that Abraham had no inheritance in Canaan because his inheritance was to be in the future: *God gave him no inheritance in it, not even enough to set his foot on. But even when Abraham had no child, He promised to give it to him for a possession, and to his descendants after him* (Acts 7:5). God used Pharaoh to bring about the promise he made to Abraham: *When the time of the promise drew near which God had sworn to Abraham, the people grew and multiplied in Egypt* (Acts 7:17).

At age seventy-five Abraham set out from Haran with his nephew Lot, and all that they had acquired together. We read that Abraham was *very rich in sheep, cattle, oxen, camels, donkeys, male and female servants besides silver and gold* (Genesis 24:35). By modern standards Abraham was a billionaire and his nephew Lot was also being blessed because of him. Between them they needed a great deal of land area to pasture their flocks and erect all of the tents needed to house their people, who were numbered in the thousands at that point.

Because of the huge flocks and herds of animals, and the constant need for large volumes of water for them and all the servants, quarrels began between Lot's men and those of Abraham. Lot should have been subservient to Abraham, at least giving him honor as his uncle and his elder, but it appears that he did not and the time soon came that the two encampments had to part ways. It became impossible for their camps to coexist with all the bickering and arguing that was going on. We now see the first of Abraham's actions that won him favor with God Almighty.

Abraham sees the inevitability of having to part company with Lot and tells him that if he goes to the left he will go to the right. Lot had gotten rich from his association with Abraham and should rightly have accepted the lower place and taken what his uncle did not choose for himself, which was his right to do so, but he did not. This was the beginning of Lot's downfall; he chose the best of all the land that he could see, the Jordan Valley, which was well watered and *was like the garden of the Lord* (Genesis 13:10).

When we take the best of everything, especially when we do not have the moral right to do so—preferring self over another more worthy of it—it will bring only trouble in this life, and Lot got his share of troubles soon enough. Lot goes off in the direction of Sodom and Gomorrah, and Abraham took the opposite path. It has been posited that Lot went Left and Abraham went Right, which is why liberals hold to the ideals of the Left and conservatives are generally more moral and hold to the higher ideals of the Right.

Lessons from Lot

Lot's misfortune, which some would say was justly deserved, showed itself first in his being taken prisoner in the war being fought between nine kings. Five kings, including the king of Sodom and the king of Gomorrah, pitted themselves in battle against four other kings of the region (Genesis 14:8–9. The battle did not fare well for the five kings, and the kings of Sodom and Gomorrah fled from the battle and hid in the hills. The four kings went their way and took with them all the people, goods, and provisions of Sodom and Gomorrah, including Lot who had been captured in the fracas along with everything he possessed. Without Abraham's protection Lot had been completely vulnerable.

When Abraham learned that his nephew had been taken captive he gathered together three hundred and eighteen of his most loyal and dedicated servants who had been born in his house, and set off in hot pursuit. Abraham caught up with the kings during the night. Abraham divided his men into two companies before attacking the kings' forces, routing them, and chasing them from the region. Abraham brought Lot and all the male and female captives, together with the plundered goods, back to Sodom.

Lot chose to live in Sodom, one of the most depraved cities on planet earth at that time. God Almighty had to rescue Lot from the divine destruction of Sodom and Gomorrah, but Lot could not convince his sons-in-law to flee from the coming disaster. There were not found ten righteous people among all the citizens of Sodom and Gomorrah (Genesis 18:32), which would have prevented the loss of thousands of lives. Lot had not been living the sort of life that he should have been, therefore no one, not even his family, looked upon him as a godly person, nor did they take his warning of impending destruction seriously. Consequently, his daughters lost their husbands because they suffered the consequences of unbelief and perished in *fire and brimstone* (Genesis 19:24). The lesson here is that we really need to be living the life we are supposed to be living in the Lord. If the candles of our faith shed light all around us, earning us the right to be taken seriously, then other people's lives may be saved *at the coming of the great and dreadful day of the Lord* (Malachi 4:5).

The angels told Lot to flee the coming holocaust, but even then he hesitated and the angels had to drag him out in order to save his life. In contrast to Abraham, who left immediately God Almighty told him, *"Get out of your country, from your family and from your father's house"* (Genesis 12:1) Lot had to be taken by the hand by angels and whined about the hardship of leaving; he asked if he could go to a place other than where the angels told him to flee to because he was afraid. When we are told by God Almighty to do something and we tell him that it will cause us inconvenience and worry and that we are afraid, we can forget about getting into a deeper walk with God anytime soon.

God gave in to Lot and allowed him to go to a small town nearby, but told them they were not to look back at the destruction. Lot's wife disobeyed and was turned into a pillar of salt. Now Lot had lost his wife as well, and all because he did not live and act the way he should have lived and acted.

The end of Lot's story insofar as we are concerned is when he gets totally drunk two nights in a row, probably because he has lost everything, that he has incestuous relationships with his two daughters. His daughters eventually give birth to two sons by their father, and those sons were Moab and Ben-Ammi, who were the ancestors of present-day Jordan, which has been another pain in the neck to Abraham's descendants, because it was the result of a work of the flesh.

I have brought Lot's story into this book, which is predominantly about Abraham's life, only as an example of what can happen when we prefer ourselves over others; are disobedient; complain when God requires us to do things that we do not want to do; and get ourselves into a situation where we commit gross sin. Remember what I said about identifying with Bible characters?

According to Your Faith

ABRAHAM had two reasons for giving Lot the best of the land that lay before them. The first is that Abraham truly believed God Almighty when he met him while he was still called Abram: *Then the Lord appeared to Abram and said, "To your descendants I will give this land." And there he built an altar to the LORD, who had appeared to him* (Genesis 12:7). Notice that the first thing Abraham did was to build and altar to the LORD, and an altar is for sacrifice and worship. It was Jesus that said, **as you have believed, so let it be done for you"** (Matthew 8:13) Something many of us need to learn about things concerning our faith is that according to our faith it will be done for us. This also works negatively as well as positively.

Abraham did not at that time have any descendants, therefore he knew the land he had given to Lot must return to him at some future date in order for it to go to his descendants. Lot was Abraham's nephew, not his descendant.

The second reason Abraham allowed Lot to take the best of the land was because it belonged to Abraham and he had the right

to give away what belonged to him. There
have only ever been two owners of the land
of Canaan. It may come as a surprise to some
readers that God Almighty owns everything
in the entire universe. His own hands created
it all, it all belongs to Him, the Bible is replete
with that fact—*God Most High, Possessor of
heaven and earth* (Genesis 14:19, 22); *The earth
is the Lord's, and all it contains, the world, and
those who dwell in it* (Psalms 24:1). *The earth
is the Lord's, and all its fullness* (1Corinthians
10:28), and so forth.

One particular day God Almighty made
a covenant with Abraham that he would
give Abraham all the land of Canaan: *On
the same day the Lord made a covenant with
Abram, saying: "To your descendants I have
given this land, **from the river of Egypt to the
great river, the River Euphrates**—the Kenites,
the Kenezzites, the Kadmonites, the Hittites,
the Perizzites, the Rephaim, the Amorites, the
Canaanites, the Girgashites, and the Jebusites"*
(Genesis 15:18–21).

Some people will no doubt think God
was being unfair in taking all that land from
under the feet of so many people and giving it
to the descendants of a single man who, at that

time, did not even have children to leave it to. But why should anyone label God Almighty as being unfair when he was only giving away what belonged to him since before Day One? Surely he is entitled to give his own possessions to whomever he so chooses? He never gave it to the *Kenites*, the *Kenezzites*, the *Kadmonites*, the *Hittites*, the *Perizzites*, the *Rephaim*, the *Amorites*, the *Canaanites*, the *Girgashites*, or the *Jebusites*—they were squatters on his land. Those peoples never gave him anything, nor did they recognize him; they all had their own sets of false gods.

Almighty God gave the land to Abraham, and after only a short period of time—after he defeated the four kings who took his nephew Lot and all the other people round about as prisoners—he, Abraham, gave to God one tenth of all the booty of the defeated armies as a tithe. Abraham gave more in one single action than all the inhabitants of the land had given throughout countless centuries. God gave the land to Abraham and received an immediate return. God has never given that land to anyone else from that day to this; it remains the property of the seed of Abraham through his son Isaac; and all the hostile Arab states, all of the Russian might, all of the U.S. State Department's hostility, and all of the world's nuclear and military might cannot alter this fact.

God is not a man, that he should lie, nor a son of man, that he should repent. Has he said, and will he not do? Or has he spoken, and will he not make it good? (Numbers 23:19). God was the owner, the possessor of the land and he saw fit to give it to Abraham, and Abraham saw fit to give the best of the land to his nephew Lot knowing that it would return to him. The principle here is that we can only give away that which we really possess. One of the great problems of the modern Church to which we belong is that preachers and teachers try to give away to congregants what they do not possess, things they have read in books, not what has been received from God Almighty. Certainly, we can give messages and teachings on what we have read in books, but edification and spiritual growth rarely takes place in hearers' lives because the message and teaching is secondhand, it has not been born of experience. One cannot give away what one has not first learned to possess through experience.

STEP OUT IN FAITH

ABRAHAM did not hold a grudge against Lot and when he first heard of Lot having been taken prisoner, he mustered men loyal to him (not "trained men") and went after the kings. Consider this and we shall see the second act that won Abraham favor with God. There are no less than four kings with their combined armies. Abraham had only three hundred and eighteen men prepared to lay down their lives in the cause of their master. We read that Jesus says no king will go out to meet another king in battle unless *he first sits down and considers whether he is able, with ten thousand men, to defeat the one coming against him with twenty thousand men* (Luke 14:31). Obviously, if he is not confident of victory he will send emissaries to ask conditions of peace while his enemy is yet a long way off. The odds against Abraham were significantly more than two to one against. It was four armies against three hundred and nineteen men (including Abraham); however, **Abraham believed God** is going to give him a son, therefore he cannot die carrying out a righteous act of rescuing a close family member.

Abraham succeeds in his mission and routs the kings and chases them out of the region. Coming back from the battle with the freed prisoners and all the goods and gold and silver, Abraham meets Melchizedek, king of Salem and priest of *God Most High, possessor of heaven and earth*, before whom Abraham *stands and lives.* Melchizedek brought out bread and wine and blessed Abraham: *And he blessed him and said: "Blessed be Abram of God Most High, Possessor of heaven and earth; and blessed be God Most High, who has delivered your enemies into your hand." And [Abraham] gave him a tithe of all* (Genesis 14:19–20).

Perhaps we should look upon the bread and the wine that Melchizedek gave Abraham as being the forerunner of what we celebrate as the Lord's Supper, because Jesus is our High Priest—*called by God **as High Priest according to the order of Melchizedek*** (Hebrews 5:10). *For this Melchizedek, king of Salem, priest of the Most High God, who met Abraham returning from the slaughter of the kings and blessed him, to whom also Abraham gave a tenth part of all, first being translated **"king of righteousness,"** and then also king of Salem, meaning **"king of peace,"** without* *father, without mother, without genealogy, having neither beginning of days nor end of life, but* **made like the Son of God,** *remains a priest continually* (Hebrews 7:-3).

Abraham's inheritance was to come through Isaac, who is also a type of Christ (we will get to this in due time) who was offered up to God as a sacrifice; now Abraham not only receives bread and wine from Melchizedek, but is also blessed by him—*Now beyond all contradiction the lesser is blessed by the greater* (Hebrews 7:7). Abraham recognizes the high calling of Melchizedek and gives him a ten percent tithe of all the spoil taken from the four kings and their troops.

The king of Sodom had returned and went out to meet the Abraham and said to him: *"Give me the persons, and take the goods for yourself"* (Genesis 14:21), but Abraham said to the king of Sodom, *"I have raised my hand to the Lord, God Most High, the Possessor of heaven and earth, that I will take nothing, from a thread to a sandal strap, and that I will not take anything that is yours,* **lest you should say, "I have made Abram rich"'** (Genesis 14:22–23). Abraham knew that it was God Almighty, and him alone, who had delivered the kings and their men into his hands, and gives to God's High Priest a tenth of all the spoils as a thanksgiving offering. Abraham would not allow anyone to think they had added to his wealth—Abraham even bought the cave of Machpelah for *four hundred shekels of silver* as a burial place for Sarah after it was offered to him for free (Genesis 23:7–16).

As mentioned previously, Abraham gave more to God Almighty in that one act through Melchizedek than all the dwellers on the land had given since time began. Abraham was a worshiper of God Almighty and as such he went through the land building altars where he worshiped God. If there is one thing the world needs today it is worshipers of God, real worshipers. The Church also has a dearth of true worshipers, it has many adherents that sing songs and go through the motions, but it lacks true worshipers. The Church is also waiting for the prophet who has dared to enter beyond the second veil and who has gazed upon that which is within—God Almighty himself.

After Abraham gave the tithe to Melchizedek, the king of Sodom asked for the souls—the people—and tells Abraham that he is welcome to the spoils. Abraham had the right to everyone and everything rescued, but Abraham was never the one to stand upon his rights. He tells the king that he would not take so much as a shoelace, not the smallest item, in case he should say that he had made Abraham rich. At no time in his life did Abraham ever say that he was a self-made man, but he did take every opportunity to make it known publicly that he was a God-made man, and he was not going to give anyone an opportunity to take away from the glory that rightly belonged to God.

What an inspiration this man Abraham should be to all of us. We need to give voluntarily from all that God has given into our hands, as an act of worship, not because someone pushes a basket under our nose and we must be seen to put something into it. How many of us magnanimously drop a dollar or two into the offering each Sunday as a way of appeasing our consciences and feel that we did God, the church, and the pastor a favor, and henceforth we are owed a return on our gesture toward the kingdom of God?

TAKE NOTHING, OWE NOTHING

ABRAHAM would take nothing from what he had retrieved from the kings with his *sword* and his *bow* in case it should be said that it had made him rich. I said earlier that Abraham was probably a billionaire by today's values, and he took three hundred and eighteen of his most loyal men, those dedicated to fight for righteousness. He did not take the young men, the old men, the wives or the children, just three hundred and eighteen men loyal to their master. The other thousand or two who made up his household were left to look after Abraham's great herds of sheep, cattle, camels, oxen and donkeys that God had given into his hand. Abraham was careful not to let anyone steal God's glory and we also should be careful not to enter into deals that may give another the opportunity to say that he made us rich. We must be careful to guard the name of our Lord by leaving no unpaid debts or hassles about money—even if we are in the right— where someone could say, "He got rich on my money."

ABRAHAM *BELIEVED*

AGAIN it must be said that Abraham was exceedingly rich and wanted for nothing, other than a son and heir to his continually growing fortune. Shortly after the meeting with Melchizedek, and refusing to take the least thing from the spoils he captured from the kings, God Almighty spoke to him again in a vision:

> *"Do not be afraid, Abram. I am your shield, your exceedingly great reward." But Abraham said, "Lord God, what will you give me, seeing I go childless, and the heir of my house is Eliezer of Damascus?" Then Abraham said, "Look, you have given me no offspring; indeed one born in my house is my heir!"*
>
> *And behold, the word of the Lord came to him, saying, "This one shall not be your heir, but **one who will come from your own body shall be your heir.**" Then he brought him outside and said, "Look now toward heaven, and count the stars if you are able to number them." And he said to him, "So shall your descendants be." And **he believed in the Lord, and he accounted it to him for righteousness***
>
> (Genesis 15:1–6).

Truly, an amazing passage. Abraham was old and had no child. Sarah his wife was not only barren, but also beyond the age of childbearing. However, Abraham **believed God** when he said that his descendants would be as the stars in the sky in number. God Almighty changed Abram's name (exalted father) to Abraham (father of a multitude): *No longer shall your name be called Abram, but your name shall be Abraham; for I have made you a father of many nations* (Genesis 17:5).

A scripture in the New Testament by James, the brother of Jesus, says it all: **Abraham believed God**, *and it was accounted to him for righteousness.* **And he was called the friend of God** (James 2:23). And speaking of the people of Israel, God says they are, *The descendants of* **Abraham my friend** (Isaiah 41:8).

When Abraham believed God rather than the impossibility of having children at his age, it was reckoned to him as righteousness. Believing against hope caused God Almighty to write "Righteous" alongside Abraham's name in *the Book of Life.* God so appreciated Abraham's belief in his words over and against the despair of the actual situation, that God chose to call him *"my friend."*

What an encouragement this should be to us. Abraham was not perfect; we have already seen how he blew it with Pharaoh king of Egypt, and again with Abimelech king of Gerar in southern Canaan, but believing God wiped Abraham's slate clean and he became God's *friend*.

If we want to be God's friend we have to believe Him against all the odds. Many will say that they believe God and believe Jesus, but their actions (or lack of them) along with the words from their lips show that if they do have belief it is only a head belief and not a heart belief. The longest journey in the world is the journey between the head and the heart.

Let me repeat one of the laws of faith that was spoken by Jesus: *as you have believed, so let it be done for you*" (Matthew 8:13). As I said earlier, this works negatively as well as positively. If you believe something could never happen, it will never happen, period.

Abraham is held up as the father of faith and is mentioned as such throughout the Bible, but effective faith can only come through thorough conviction. And Abraham was thoroughly convinced that God would keep his promise, and being convinced he acted on his convictions and became God's friend—he was **fully persuaded that God had power to do what he had promised** (Romans 4:21). The good news is that all who truly believe God are blessed with *the faith of Abraham* (Romans 4:6) and that faith is reckoned to us as righteousness. It is the good news of salvation through Jesus—*in it the righteousness of God is revealed from faith to faith; as it is written, "**The righteous shall live by faith**"* (Romans 1:17). Salvation of our souls is everything, *which is through **faith in Christ**, the **righteousness which is from God by faith*** (Philippians 3:9).

The word *faith* is used two hundred and twenty-seven times in the New Testament. Obviously, it is the most important component of salvation. Faith and belief are synonymous, you cannot have one without the other: *without **faith** it is impossible to please him, for he who comes to God **must believe** that **he is**, and that he is a rewarder of those **who diligently seek** him* (Hebrews 11:6). Enough said.

If you do not have the faith to truly believe that Jesus is *God's only begotten Son* and that he died in order that you may live, then as Jesus said, *"According to your faith let it be to you"* (Matthew 9:29).

THE DISCIPLINE OF OBEDIENCE

IN due time Abraham's son Isaac was born, and Abraham loved him. Somewhere in Isaac's years, between twenty and thirty, Abraham is told to take Isaac and offer him *as a burnt offering* on a mountain in the land of Moriah. God was testing Abraham, and said to him, *"Abraham!" And he said, "Here I am." Then he said, "Take now your son, your only son Isaac, whom you love, and go to the land of Moriah, and offer him there as a burnt offering on one of the mountains of which I shall tell you"* (Genesis 22:1–2).

God said *"now"* to Abraham, and God says *"now"* to us, and when God says *"now,"* he does not mean presently, or when we feel like it. Concerning the covenant of circumcision that God made with Abraham, we are told than Abraham circumcised the flesh of their foreskins with a crude flint knife *that very day, as God had said to him* (Genesis 17:23). By the discipline of obedience we get to the place where Abraham was, and then we see who God is, and see him in all of his wonder and majesty. The thing that set Abraham apart was that he was prepared to do anything for God, and that he did it right away.

How many reading this never got baptized I wonder? God says *"Repent, Believe, and **be Baptized**,"* in that order. **Repent, and** *let every one of you **be baptized** in the name of Jesus Christ **for the remission of sins**; and you shall receive **the gift of the Holy Spirit*** (Acts 2:38). *And now why are you waiting? Arise and **be baptized, and wash away your sins**, calling on the name of the Lord* (Acts 22:16). I do not believe that baptism is going to affect your salvation, but I guarantee that disobedience is going to affect your relationship with God. I use baptism here merely as an example, not because I am a crusader for baptism. Many times God will say *"Now"* and we say **"Later!"** Obedience is a discipline.

TAKE NOW YOUR SON

GOD says to Abraham, *"Take **now** your only son Isaac."* Ishmael, remember, is not recognized because he was a work of the flesh, and as I said earlier, "No work of the flesh is recognized by God and Ishmael was not recognized as Abraham's heir. Works of the flesh are a pain in God's heart and a pain in mankind's neck." So we read that Abraham *rose early in the morning*, saddled the donkey, took two young men and set off for the land of Moriah.

Do we ever pause to think what may have passed through Abraham's mind about taking his son, the son of promise, and to offer him as a burnt offering? That Abraham *rose early in the morning* and set off for Moriah tells us what he wrestled with that night. **Abraham believed God** that he would be the father of a multitude. **Abraham believed God** that the land of Canaan was given in perpetuity to him and his descendants through the line of Isaac: **In Isaac your seed shall be called** (Genesis 21:12). Therefore, in Abraham's reasoning, if he killed Isaac by offering him as a burnt sacrifice, God Almighty must raise Isaac from the dead, and we see that this is his reasoning because he said to the men who went with him to Moriah: *"Stay here with the donkey while I and the boy go over there. **We will worship** and then **we will come back to you**"* (Genesis 22:5). To Abraham, the sacrifice of his only son, through whom the promises must come, was simply an act of ***worship***!

What an incredible man! Abraham gives a tenth of all the spoil to the Priest of God Most High, and considers it worship. He sacrifices animals and considers it worship, and now he is going to sacrifice his only son as an act of worship.

I mentioned earlier that Isaac was a type of Christ, and we should therefore notice that it was **on the third day** (Genesis 22:4) that Abraham arrived at Mount Moriah—the same Mount Moriah on which Jesus was crucified. Abraham then says to the young men that he and Isaac **will go and worship**, and <u>**we will return**</u> to you. There is the proof of Abraham's belief in the resurrection of the dead, because Abraham said to his young men, *"Stay here with the donkey; the lad and I will go yonder and worship, and **we will come back** to you"* (Genesis 22:4).

Isaac was not the little child that we see in kiddies' story books. He is, as mentioned before, somewhere between twenty and thirty years of age. Abraham was *one hundred years old when Isaac was born* (Genesis 21:5). Therefore Abraham was between one hundred and twenty and one hundred and thirty years old, whereas Isaac was in his prime and could easily have overpowered Abraham while he was being bound as a sacrifice. But had not God said of Abraham: *"I have chosen him,* **that he may command his children and his household after him to keep the way of the Lord by doing righteousness and justice,** *so that the Lord may bring to Abraham what he has promised him"* (Genesis 18:19).

God Almighty chose Abraham for two reasons, the first being that **Abraham believed God**—he believed God even when reality screamed—"Impossible!"

Secondly, God chose Abraham because he would command his children and his whole household to keep the way of the Lord. God is looking for people who believe in him, and who will raise their children and their households to keep the way of faith in God, and who will walk in and practice *righteousness and justice.*

In complete contrast to King David, God Almighty chose Abraham because he could *command his children and his household to keep the way of the Lord.* How desperately we need fathers today who will command their children and their households to keep the way of the Lord. Crime runs rampant throughout the Western world for the lack of fathers who will command their children to keep the way of the Lord. Isaac submitted to being bound because he loved, respected and obeyed his God-fearing father. Most readers will know the end of the story, how God was only testing Abraham and prevented him from harming Isaac. God had a ram conveniently caught up in a thicket, which was then offered as a sacrifice in the place of Isaac. And again, like Jesus after his ascension, Isaac has no physical interaction with us again until he comes to meet with his bride (Genesis 24:63–66. (For a full exposition of the magnitude of the actions of Abraham and Isaac on Mount Moriah— perhaps the greatest of Christendom's overlooked and misunderstood prophecies— see page 110 and the corresponding **Endnote 16** in my book *No Other Name*.)

Faith secures a Bride

When Abraham was old (Sarah having died some five years beforehand), he felt that it was time for Isaac to be married, but Isaac's marriage had to be in harmony with the blessing God had bestowed upon Abraham and his descendants. Abraham refused to allow his son to have a wife from among the Canaanites. Abraham made his chief servant, Eliezer, put his hand under his thigh and *swear that he would not take a wife from among the Canaanites for Isaac* (Genesis 24:3). Neither would Abraham allow Isaac to leave Canaan, the land God Almighty had bequeathed him, to seek a bride from Abraham's people (Genesis 24:6). Instead he made his most trusted servant swear a solemn oath and then sent him to Abraham's own country and family in Mesopotamia, to bring back a wife for Isaac.

Abraham's rationale was that Isaac was not merely a wealthy, godly, eligible candidate for marriage, but that he must never marry into any of the families of the Canaanites whose possession he would ultimately inherit for posterity.

Abraham had absolute faith that God Almighty would lead Eliezer to his people and secure a wife for Isaac. Abraham told Eliezer: *God will **send His angel before you**, and you shall take a wife for my son from there* (Genesis 24:7). And God did exactly that. Eliezer *the servant took ten of his master's camels and departed, for all his master's goods were in his* *hand. And he arose and went to Mesopotamia, to the city of Nahor* (Genesis 24:10). Abraham's servant arrived in Mesopotamia *and he made his camels kneel down outside the city by a well of water at evening time, the time when women go out to draw water.* Eliezer prayed that his master's God would bring him success in his quest and show him the right girl, the one whom Isaac would take as a wife.

Eliezer specifically prayed:

*"See, here I stand by the well of water, and the daughters of the men of the city are coming out to draw water. Now **let it be that the young woman to whom I say, 'Please let down your pitcher that I may drink,' and she says, 'Drink, and I will also give your camels a drink'—let her be the one you have appointed for your servant Isaac.** And by this I will know that you have shown kindness to my master"*

(Genesis 24:13–14).

Rebekah, the beautiful virgin daughter of Abraham's brother, was the first to come to the well, she came just as Eliezer finished praying his prayer. He asked for a drink of water from her pitcher and Rebekah said:

"Drink, my lord." *Then she quickly let her pitcher down to her hand, and gave him a drink. And when she had finished giving him a drink, she said, "I will draw water for your camels also, until they have finished drinking"* (Genesis 24:18–19).

Eliezer remained silent as Rebekah ran back and forth with her pitcher full of water from the well to the trough for the camels, Eliezer was waiting in order to be certain that Rebekah was the right girl. When she finished watering his camels he gave her gifts of gold—a nose ring and bracelets, betrothing her to Isaac—and bowed down and worshiped, saying, *"Blessed be the Lord God of my master Abraham, who has not forsaken his mercy and his truth toward my master. As for me, being in the way, the Lord led me to the house of my master's brethren"* (Genesis 24:27). Of course, the story had a happy-ever-after ending, and that is when we next read of Isaac as he *brought her into his mother Sarah's tent;* ***and he took Rebekah and she became his wife, and he loved her*** (Genesis 24:67).

Abraham had absolute faith that God would show Eliezer the right virgin maid from among his own people, and God deliberately arranged events so that Eliezer would select Rebekah. Faith that is sure of God is the only faith there is. And Abraham's faith in God Almighty had rubbed off on his servant Eliezer who went out on a limb to correctly identify the virgin girl for his master's son. God Almighty chose Abraham *that he may command his children and his household after him to keep the way of the Lord*, and the actions of Eliezer, who was born in Abraham's house, show the wisdom of God's choice. There is a moral here for us in the story of Abraham, Eliezer, Isaac, and Rebekah: Faith, trust and piety will move mountains of obstacles that stand in the way of God's perfect will for us.

FAITH AS OPPOSED TO LEGALISM

JAMES, the brother of Jesus, tells us that a man is justified by works and not just by faith alone:

> *Was not Abraham our father justified by works when he offered Isaac his son on the altar? Do you see that **faith was working together with his works, and by works faith was made perfect**? And the Scripture was fulfilled which says,*

*"**Abraham believed God, and it was accounted to him for righteousness.**" And **he was called the friend of God.** You see then that **a man is justified by works, and not by faith only.** ... For as the body without the spirit is dead, so **faith without works is dead** also* (James 2:21–24, 26).

James is saying that justification comes not just through faith alone, but also by actions that are in full accordance with that faith. Do not believe for one moment that James was a legalist, as some say. Either the Bible is inspired or it is not. Either we believe the whole Book or none of it. We do not have the right to take out of the Bible that which does not fit our own particular theology. Some say that the Apostle Paul had a thing about women. Paul had a thing about the blood of Christ and a host of other things. If he was wrong about women then it follows that he was probably wrong about everything else.

It was not only James who taught that faith requires actions. Jesus had much to say about that subject in parables, in different words, but with the same intent. Following is one of several discourses:

When the Son of Man comes in his glory, and all the holy angels with him, then he will sit on the throne of his glory. All the nations will be gathered before him, and he will separate them one from another, **as a shepherd divides his sheep from the goats.** *And he will set the sheep on his right hand, but the goats on the left. Then the King will say to those on his right hand, "Come, you blessed of my Father, inherit the kingdom prepared for you from the foundation of the world: for* **I was hungry and you gave me food; I was thirsty and you gave me drink; I was a stranger and you took me in; I was naked and you clothed me; I was sick and you visited me; I was in prison and you came to me.'**

"Then the **righteous** *will answer him, saying, 'Lord, when did we see you hungry and feed you, or thirsty and give you drink? When did we see you a stranger and take you in, or naked and clothe you? Or when did we see you sick, or in prison, and come to you?' And the King will answer and say to them, "Assuredly, I* **say to you, inasmuch as you did it to one of the least of these my brethren, you did it to Me.'**

"*Then he will also say to those on the left hand, 'Depart from me, you cursed,* **into the everlasting fire prepared for the devil and his angels**: *for* **I was hungry and you gave me no food; I was thirsty and you gave me no drink; I was a stranger and you did not take me in, naked and you did not clothe me, sick and in prison and you did not visit me.'**

"*Then they also will answer him, saying, 'Lord, when did we see you hungry or thirsty or a stranger or naked or sick or in prison, and did not minister to you?' Then he will answer them, saying, "Assuredly,* **I say to you, inasmuch as you did not do it to one of the least of these, you did not do it to me.'** *And these will go away into everlasting punishment, but the* **righteous** *into eternal life* (Matthew 25:31–46).

Paul wrote the following, but it would just as easily have fitted into the teachings of Jesus:

Therefore, my beloved, as you have always obeyed, not as in my presence only, but now much more in my absence, **work out your own salvation with fear and trembling** (Philippians 2:12).

Most Christians have a distorted view of Christianity, they have a passive religion, but pure and undefiled religion is active:

Pure and undefiled religion before God and the Father is this: to **visit orphans and widows in their trouble, and to keep oneself unspotted from the world**
                              (James 1:27).

Justification by faith is true, but it is only half true, like Sarah being the sister of Abraham. It is only half of the coin, and half of a coin buys nothing. We must have the other half of the coin if it is to be of value. Some will remember the story of Zacchaeus the rich, chief tax collector. Jesus was passing through Jericho and Zacchaeus heard the uproar, but could not see above the heads of the people because he was short in stature. He ran ahead and climbed up into a Sycamore-fig tree to get a better view. Jesus looked up at Zacchaeus, calls him by name and tells him to come down because he is going to stay with him that night.

Zacchaeus is more than a little impressed and immediately believes Jesus is the Christ, *the Coming One* (Luke 7:19). The people, like many Christians today, were not happy because Jesus was going to stay with a *"sinner."* Right away Zacchaeus says, *"Behold, Lord, the* ***half of my goods I give to the poor.*** *And if I have* ***defrauded anyone*** *of anything, I* ***restore it fourfold"*** (Luke 19:8), and Jesus says in response: *"Today salvation has come to this house, since* ***he also is a son of Abraham"*** (Luke 19:9).

Jesus did not mean what some commentators would have us to believe, that Zacchaeus was also a Jew. Of course Zachaeus was a Jew, that is not the point, the point is that Zacchaeus **believed** Jesus and immediately acted upon his belief by declaring that he was giving away half his money and goods—and he was rich—and would recompense with four times the amount anything he had defrauded people of. This was the reaction of a true believer in Jesus.

The Pharisees said to Jesus, *"Abraham is our father"* (John 8:39). And Jesus said to them: ***"If you were Abraham's children, you would do the works of Abraham"*** (John 8:39). It is that simple. Those who have the faith of Abraham do the works of Abraham. Those who do not do the works of Abraham do not have the faith of Abraham. Those who do not have the faith of Abraham do not have a place in the kingdom of God.

Throughout the Bible we read many examples of feats of faith—of an abundance of wondrous miracles performed through men and women of faith. However, God Almighty makes it perfectly clear to us: *I am the Lord, I do not change* (Malachi 3:6), thus we can safely assume and rely on the fact that, if God is the same as he has always been, and will always be what he has always been, he will today act the same way with every man and every woman who manifests the same degree of faith that those of yesterday did.

RELATIONSHIP WITH GOD SHOWS ITSELF IN SEPARATION

I ask my readers this question: "Do you want to be a friend of God?" If you answer "Yes," then you must do the works of Abraham. Believe God and act accordingly. Live like you believe God. Do you believe God when he says the only way to save your life is to lose it? Then you must lose it—*if* you want to save it!

The real Christian feels no more at home in this world than Abraham did when he set out from Ur for the land of Canaan. If he spoke the language he spoke it with an accent—he was called *Abraham the Hebrew* (Genesis 14:13)—they all knew he was not one of them. Personal relationship with God in the Old Testament showed itself in separation, and this is symbolized by Abraham's separation from his country and from his kith and kin. And Abraham's faith separated him from those around him, he was first naturally (physically) separated and then spiritually separated: *It is not the spiritual that is first but the natural, and then the spiritual* (1Corinthians 15:46). We are also to be naturally and spiritually separated from the world.

Jesus says in John 15:14, *"You are my friends **if you do whatever** I command you."* And he commanded us to *love one another* and *forgive one another* (not just those who are Christians). He says that we are to feed the hungry, clothe the naked, take in the homeless. To place our light where all can see it and glorify the Father in heaven by our good works—the works of Abraham. Jesus said that all the Law and the Prophets hung on loving God and loving our neighbor. Abraham cared for the welfare of strangers and provided them with water for their feet and food and drink for their sustenance (Genesis 18:1–5). He also cared for lost souls: As the two angels went toward the doomed cities of Sodom and Gomorrah, Abraham went near and stood before the LORD, interceding for the people of Sodom and Gomorrah (Genesis 18:23–33).

If you want to be a *friend of God*, then act like you know Him.

It is interesting to note that in the Book of Genesis, God said to Abraham (when he was ninety-nine years old and still called Abram): *"I am Almighty God; walk before me and be blameless"* (Genesis 17:1). The word *"blameless"* is often translated as *"perfect,"* but the Hebrew word used is the same root as "duplicate," or "replica," or "double," the only difference being a single vowel. What God said to Abraham, he says to us also: **"Walk before me and be a reflection of me."**

Do you want to know Him? Believe the Bible and **the words of the Amen, the faithful and true witness, the beginning of the creation of God.** (Revelation 3:14).

The distinguishing mark of Abraham's life was that he was *fully persuaded that, what God had promised, God was able to perform*

(Romans 4:21). And there, in a nutshell, you have Abraham's *raison d'être*!

RAMON BENNETT, the author of this book, also writes the *Update*, the regular newsletter of the *Arm of Salvation Ministries*. The *Update* keeps readers informed on world events that affect Israel, and also, on the ministry of Ramon Bennett and his wife, Zipporah. An annual donation of $20.00 is requested for the *Update*, which is *available only* by e-mail in digital PDF format. Subscriptions to the *Update* and any love gifts should be made via PayPal: <*payments@ shekinahbooks.com*>.

Arm of Salvation (AOS) was founded by Ramon Bennett in 1980 and is an indigenous Israeli ministry that is dependent upon gifts and the proceeds from its book and music sales to sustain its work in and for Israel and the Jewish people. These are critical times for Israel so financial support is appreciated.

Copies of *Abe* and other books by Ramon Bennett (see following pages) are all available from *Amazon.com*.

Albums of popular Hebrew worship songs composed by Zipporah Bennett, are available by contacting Zipporah at the following e-mail address: <*usa@shekinahbooks.com*>.

Visit the website:
http://www.shekinahbooks.com
to subscribe, and/or donate via PayPal.

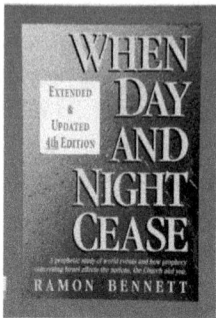

fourth edition

"WHEN DAY & NIGHT CEASE is the most comprehensive, factual and informative book on Israel—past, present and future. If you want a true picture of how Israel is falling into Bible prophecy today, look no further. You will want to read this book"

324 pages – Paperback, or Kindle e-book

PHILISTINE 2 is the newly updated edition of the blockbuster 1995 original. It lays bare the Arab mind, Islam, the Koran, the United Nations, the news media, rewritten history, and the Israeli-PLO peace accord. *PHILISTINE* will grip you. *PHILISTINE* will inform you. *PHILISTINE* will shock you. Until you read *PHILISTINE* you will never understand the Middle East—the world's most volatile region.

364 pages – Paperback, or Kindle e-book

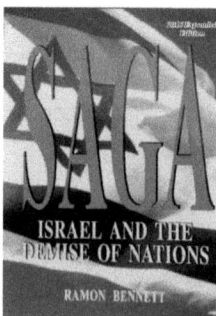

SAGA: UNDERSTAND the chaos taking place around the world today! *SAGA* shows that Jews died because cruelty and evil and anti-Semitism are not confined to one race or nation, but are found everywhere. *SAGA* is about Israel and Israel's God; about war and judgment—past, present, and future. Nations came and went, empires rose and fell; and God is still judging nations today. A "must read" in light of world events today.

284 pages – Paperback, or Kindle e-book

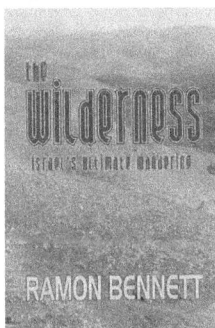

THE WILDERNESS: "*VERY INFORMATIVE BOOK FOR THOSE WHO* are looking for answers to what is happening in the middle east. God's Word is truth and Ramon Bennett breaks down verses that I've wondered about for years. A very good read, you won't be able to put it down."

— William D. Douglas

335 pages – Paperback, or Kindle e-book

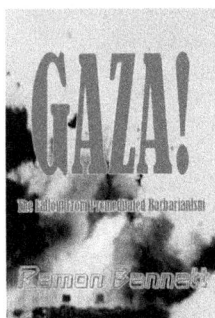

GAZA!: An accurate account of the events that led up to, and took place during, Israel's Operation Protective Edge, the 50-day war against Hamas in Gaza in 2014. It is a factual account of what took place, when it took place, why it took place, and the result of it having taken place. .

134 pages – Paperback, or Kindle e-book

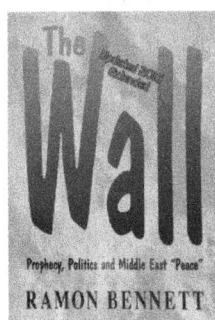

THE WALL: "They lead My people astray, saying 'Peace!' when there is no peace" (Ezekiel 13:10).

The Wall exposes the Israel-Arab peace process for what it is, an attempt to break Israel down "piece" by "piece." This book contains information the mainstream media, the CIA, the White House, and others would rather you did not know.

367 pages – Paperback, or Kindle e-book

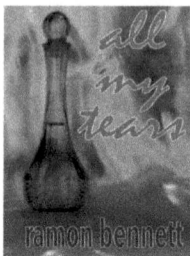

RAMON BENNETT has been introduced as "someone who has suffered the trials of Job."

Often verging on the unbelievable, **ALL MY TEARS** is Ramon's astounding autobiographical testimony; a story of an unwanted, abused child whom God adopted and anointed, and uses around the world for His glory.

448 pages – Paperback, or Kindle e-book

HISTORY, the gospels of Matthew, Mark, Luke, and John blended together in a ground-breaking uninterrupted read.

The **Color Print Edition** shows from where each interpolated piece comes from. Bible Students find this book fascinating. A Black Print Edition also available.

184 pages – Paperback, or Kindle e-book

No Other Name: An edifying and informational feast for students of the Bible. Some of the more obscure sayings of Jesus are dealt with in Endnote expositions (mini Bible Studies) by the author throughout his ground-breaking continuous gospel narrative.

292 pages – Paperback, or Kindle e-book

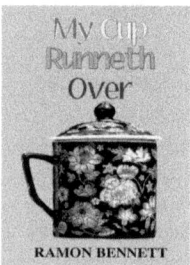

My Cup Runneth Over is a call to arms! The Western Church stands at a crossroads, it is dying for lack of zeal and love for Jesus. Materialism and lust for "things" are choking it. All-too-comfortable Christians profess to believe in Jesus, but deny Him by their silence and passivity. The Church must return to 1st-Century basics like faith and belief in a miracle working God. Effective faith results from absolute conviction.

72 pages – Paperback, or Kindle e-book

__BOOK & MUSIC BY ZIPPORAH BENNETT__

Return, Daughter of Zion!

Zipporah Bennett's testimony and autobiography. Read how Zipporah, a God-hungry Orthodox Jewish girl, found the Reality she longed for. This book, often amusing, will help the reader better understand the way Jewish people think and feel about the "Christian" Jesus.

137 pages – Paperback, or Kindle

SHEKINAH

Available on *Amazon.com*

Hebrew worship from one of Israel's foremost composers of Messianic worship songs

Hallelu	*Kuma Adonai*	*Mi Ha'amin?*
		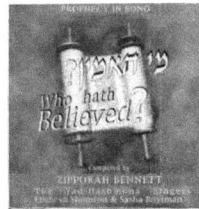
"Hallelu" – Dual Hebrew–English songs of worship	*"Arise O Lord!"* Songs of warfare and worship	*"Who Hath Believed?"* Hebrew and Aramaic prophecies in song

For a descriptive overview or to purchase the above CD albums go to:

http://www.shekinahbooks.com

All books advertised in these pages are available from *Amazon.com*

www.ingramcontent.com/pod-product-compliance
Lightning Source LLC
Chambersburg PA
CBHW060722030426
42337CB00017B/2974